Social Finance

An Introduction to the Future of Finance

Garon Agrawal, Melvin Joseph, Shiva Dave

Copyright © 2023 by Financitive

Visit the author's website at www.financitive.org.

All rights reserved.

No portion of this book may be reproduced in any form without written permission from the publisher or author, except as permitted by U.S. copyright law.

This publication is designed to provide accurate and authoritative information in regard to the subject matter covered. It is sold with the understanding that neither the author nor the publisher is engaged in rendering legal, investment, accounting, or other professional services. While the publisher and author have used their best efforts in preparing this book, they make no representations or warranties with respect to the accuracy or completeness of the contents of this book and specifically disclaim any implied warranties of merchantability or fitness for a particular purpose. No warranty may be created or extended by sales representatives or written sales materials. The advice and strategies contained herein may not be suitable for your situation. You should consult with a professional when appropriate. Neither the publisher nor the author shall be liable for any loss of profit or any other commercial damages, including but not limited to special, incidental, consequential, personal, or other damages.

First edition 2023

Table of Contents

Preface: Our Story 5

Overview of Social Finance 7
    Definitions and History 9
    Aspects: Investments, Policies, Innovations, and Initiatives 12
    ESG 16
    Sustainable Development Goals 18
    Why it Matters 22

Application and Impact 25
    Global Transition and Impact 27
    Diversity, Equity, and Inclusion Investing 30
    Impact Bonds: Communities and Poverty Alleviation 33
    Microfinance 36
    Crowdfunding and Angel Investing 39
    Green Finance and Environmental Impact 41

Case Studies 43
    Women's World Banking 45
    Ecology Building Society 48
    Triodos Bank: Netherland's First Social Bank ... 50
    Accion Micro-Credit 52

The Future Ahead 55

- Social Entrepreneurship and Bank 57
- Private and Public Sector 59
- Current and Future Challenges 61
- Cryptocurrency and Blockchain 63

Getting Involved 67

- Personal Finance 69
- Careers 71
- Institutions and Enterprises 73
- Taking Initiative 75

Authors' Note 77

Glossary 79

Preface: Our Story

The idea for this book was the result of many ideas. This book is the first of many goals and projects for our organization, Financitive. At Financitive, our organization embodies the ideal intersection of finance and initiative, hence the name. But before discovering our passion for social finance, we were three students who believed in the power of financial literacy in helping individuals, families, and organizations to take control and improve their economic well-being. After countless hours of discussion and brainstorming, though, we realized that we collectively envisaged something that could improve lives in a financial sense and harness the power of financial products and services to achieve a positive impact in the global movement to meet Sustainable Development Goals and more. The term encapsulating our vision, we found, was known as social finance.

The coining of the term exemplified the global efforts to take steps in the right direction, even in a field that historically prioritized returns as the core indicator of value. Nonetheless, the fact that none of us, even as young finance enthusiasts, had encountered the term or any of its counterparts was something we couldn't ignore. Social finance was the future of global finance, yet our students—our future leaders, activists, economists, and more—weren't exposed to the field to the extent of other areas. It wasn't even close. We realized we had to address this issue, and thus Financitive was born.

Financitive had a mission to educate students about the future of social finance through content, social media, events, and a community of like-minded finance enthusiasts. However, our social media and website engagement was slow initially. The enthusiasm for students to volunteer after our announcements revealed that even exposure could be highly consequential. Exposure wasn't our ultimate goal, though, for we aspired to equip students with the passion and knowledge of social finance to create a foundation for their future initiatives and endeavors. In turn, we started writing articles for our website that would help introduce students to the field and its components. That process led us to discover our love for writing about this topic and a problem in our approach.

In social finance, we had to build up interest practically from scratch. There was no motive or foundation in place for students to even search for our website, or other social finance resources, for that matter. Social finance had to be brought to communities. Specifically, it had to be brought to schools and classrooms. Naturally, we figured a book would be the perfect project to address this goal, mainly an introductory text, since most current social finance books cater to corporations, executives, and governments.

We hope that this book will help us achieve our goals and realize our vision and provide you with the foundation and drive to pursue your dream, especially those related to social entrepreneurship and impact. This book is designed to be an introduction and just touch briefly on each topic. For a deeper dive, we recommend visiting our website, footnotes provided throughout the book, and the suggested readings at the end. Although this book is an introduction to social finance, it is an introduction to the result you will leave in this field or others.

Overview of Social Finance

Definitions and History

Social Finance or sustainable finance funds environmental, social, and cultural changes to increase profitability. Social Finance began in the early 1900s after the promotion of modern-day capitalism and a free market world in the 1800s. People understood the potential of being able to solve real-world problems like climate change, racial disputes, and more while empowering the growing economy. Some aspects of social finance like microfinance, providing financial services to low-income individuals or groups who are typically excluded from traditional banking, started far prior to social finance's emergence. Some social finance aspects like SRI, socially responsible investing, became popularized after the 2008 financial crash despite having existed for decades.

The crash caused a demand for more ethically responsible investing due to a lack of trust in the financial sector. Since then, many governments have started to implement social finance into their economy by regulating greenhouse gas emissions to reduce environmental impact or pushing companies to service a diverse clientele by demanding more transparent reporting. These regulations have set a standard for many companies setting goals to reach Net Zero by 2050. Reaching Net Zero means the company won't produce greenhouse gas themselves and neither will the companies they work with. In addition to this, many Social Finance aspects have gained momentum, including:

- Social Impact Bonds - using lent money to promote social initiatives.

- Socially Responsible Investing - an investment strategy where investors research a company's ethical practices as well as environmental and social impact to determine if they're a sustainable investment.

- Value-Based Investing - an investment strategy where investors invest into companies that align with their values such as: focusing on environmental impact, promoting racial equality, and women's rights.

- Triple Bottom Line - A method of business focused on its impact on people and the planet just as much as making a profit.

- ESG Reporting - a policy requiring companies to disclose their environmental and social impact. Some impact investors use these disclosures to determine whether or not to invest in a company.

- Social Investment Funds - a pool of funds from investors to fund non-profits and/or sustainable projects.

Having a healthy ESG can feasibly improve a company's profitability, though the implementation of these strategies is costly, nonetheless. Thus, although profitability is not guaranteed, we may choose to be less profitable in order to achieve a positive impact on our planet. That said, some elementary examples of profitability include:

- If a beach resort helps fund cleaner ocean initiatives, their hotel will attract more guests because the ocean will be cleaner and safer to swim in.

- If a shoe company supports local running and cross-country teams, the athletes will run in their shoes instead of competitors as well as receive promotion from athletes being pictured wearing their shoes.

- If a company has a diverse employee base and board, it will be able to generate more ideas because of the different backgrounds and experiences, leading to profitability through innovation.

Aspects: Investments, Policies, Innovations, and Initiatives

The field of Social Finance spreads across many different sectors, from finance and law to engineering and sciences. But, for each of these sectors to run, they need a financial foundation. Finance is helpful because all things need funding and need to make a profit. We will cover the four aspects of Social Finance, and each has separate ideals, revenue methods, and funding structures.

In Social Finance investments, two groups of people make a profit, investors, and institutions. It begins with the investor, an individual, organization, or fund looking to create profit through their investment. They invest in social finance institutions through an intermediary, bond, or exchange.

- Intermediaries are regulators, trade groups, or service providers that make connecting investors to financial institutions more accessible. They help investors discover, transfer funds, and aid in the investing process.

- Bonds are a method of fundraising where the investor loans the organization money for a percentage back, also called the coupon rate, at the end of the bond term.

- Exchanges are where you can buy individual stocks or ETFs. Most countries have an exchange. For example, you can buy SoFi Technologies Inc[1]. under the stock ticker SOFI on the Nasdaq exchange. Many exchanges exist, typically one for every country, but there are also impact-driven capital exchange platforms that work to promote social and environmental change.

They use Green investing, sometimes called ethical investing, an investment strategy where investors invest in ESG-supportive organizations. These investments can grow over time due to the company's expansion leading to higher stock prices and increasing the investor's portfolio value. Social Finance institutions make money through investments too. When investors invest in the institution, the institution uses the money to fund various green initiatives. SoFi Technologies Inc. is a financial institution. They act as a middleman between the investor and the social finance enterprises. Eventually, those green initiatives turn a profit. These initiatives generate income in various ways. For example, wind farms profit by selling energy to households or utility companies. Families typically use it to live on while utility companies sell it back to the power grid to power other homes. The profit eventually goes back to the investor in the form of loan repayment and added interest.

Policies are another aspect of Social Finance that is very crucial. One of the policies that are currently still being worked on is social impact bonds. Social impact bonds, often called Pay-For-Success, are government bonds that fund ESG issues. Investors can invest in these bonds. They tend to be rather risky because investors won't make any money if the

1   SoFi Technologies Inc. https://www.sofi.com/

bond falls through and fails to complete the social finance initiative. Additionally, due to these bonds being so new, most bond issuers don't have a history of reliability making them lowered-grade investments. So, typically investors invest purely in the hope of concluding an ESG issue. But, if the fund is successful, typically the country's government repays investors. There are many issues social impact bonds work to solve; a few are: Supporting immigrants, Supporting the homeless, Green energy initiatives, and Habitat restoration. Social impact bonds are started and completed through 5 steps.

1. Identifying the Issue: Governments work with intermediaries to progress toward an objective.

2. Fundraise and Planning: They work with investors to raise funding and plan out an initiative.

3. Follow Through: They implement the agenda for the affected community and provide help solving the issue.

4. Measure Results: Finally, if the project succeeds, the investors are repaid their principal as well as interest.

28 countries have created over 150+ social impact bonds. At the same time, policies to develop more transparency with ESG are being made. The SEC (Security and Exchange Commission) is working to create policies making ESG reports mandatory and transparent.

Many innovations have been made in the Social Finance industry. Both innovations promote social finance awareness as well as ESG innovations. Due to social finance being a little-known topic, raising awareness is a severe problem. Companies like the Rockefeller Foundation are pioneers in raising social finance awareness. They were one of the first places to implement ESG strategies like hiring diverse people to help give problems new perspectives. They also worked to promote social impact bonds. Lastly, they raised 40 million dollars for social finance initiatives. ESG innovations are essential too. With more and more companies adopting ESG policies, the workplace is becoming more efficient. It's been shown that having a diverse employee set, supporting environmental issues, and listening to your customers improves profitability, "Companies with racially and ethnically diverse leadership and executive teams have a 35% higher likelihood of financially outperforming companies with little or no diversity." Luckily, now the majority of companies publish ESG reports because of policies and investors pushing for more transparency.

So many issues fall under the social finance category: Water conservation, reduced energy expenditure, refugee displacement, diversity, and more. Many non-profits fall under the social finance category without even intending. Social Finance deserves more attention because of the urgent issues needing to be solved through innovations in money and capital markets. The industry is off to a great start, but the sooner these problems are solved, the more equal, clean, and developed the world can be environmentally, socially, and economically.

ESG

The ESG (environmental, social, and corporate governance) is a set of criteria for assessing firms based on ecological activism and sustainability-related risks. It is used to screen investments based on the extent to which a firm's policies are aligned with the ESG's three elementary/primary facets: environmental, social, and corporate governance. The ecological aspect focuses on sustainability and preservation and is used to prevent firms from overexploiting natural resources. Its social part focuses on people and relationships. The third aspect, governance, focuses on corporate governance and changing how organizations have been governed in the past.

The environmental aspect is focused on preserving the natural world. These are actions unsustainable to the environment in the long run, such as greenhouse gas emissions, deforestation, pollution, and climate change, depleting natural resources, among others. In turn, firms dependent on these have become unattractive. The social aspect pertains to inclusion, gender equality, racial equality, and worker rights, along with movements to increase customer satisfaction and employee engagement as well as a code of ethics within organizations. Diversity is believed to grow the pool of talent from which a firm can employ its workers. It also evaluates firms using child labor, exploiting consumers, animal welfare, and factors into CSR (Corporate Social Responsibility). Due to the rise of ESG, more and more firms are being penalized for violating these rights.

Governance refers to the decision-making aspect from policymaking to the distribution of rights and responsibilities among different participants in corporations, including the board of directors, managers, shareholders, and stakeholders. It is one of the essential aspects considering the vast impact it has on the firm's policies and actions, which can lead to an equally significant effect on the world depending on the size and magnitude of the firms. Poor corporate governance is visible in the Volkswagen emissions test scandal, where Volkswagen violated the Clean Air Act as the vehicles were equipped with "defeat devices" in the form of computer software designed to cheat on federal emissions tests. Or Facebook's misuse of data could have severe implications for society and the environment.

ESG has been shown to encourage responsible investment. It compels firms to act in ethically sound ways by punishing/penalizing them if they violate any policies. It may bolster sustainability in the long term and further worker rights.

Sustainable Development Goals

Human Societies are causing more and more damage to the environment and, in turn, the world's sustainability than ever before. Since the advent of the industrial revolution, we have prioritized immense wealth over the existence of our planet, as we eradicate forests for farms and factories, devour the life essence of oceans, and destroy massive habitats, all while making the life of the average human miserable as inflation rises and inequality runs rampant.

The last decade has been the hottest recorded; sea levels are rising at the fastest rate in 3,000 years, while more than 800 million people are already vulnerable to climate change impacts. Furthermore, more than 700 million people live in extreme poverty, on less than USD 2 per day; there are more than 152 million cases of child labor globally, and an estimated 821 million people were undernourished in 2017, in addition to the environmental problems.

Our social fabric is on the verge of being torn apart while the very existence of our planet is uncertain. This is where Sustainable Development Goals offer hope in these challenging times, proposing solutions to save the world, conserve nature, and create a prosperous future for humanity. SDGs lay out 17 goals to address and end some of society's most significant problems, aiming at poverty, protecting the planet, and ensuring that all people enjoy peace and prosperity.

The 17 Sustainable goals are:

GOAL 1: No Poverty

GOAL 2: Zero Hunger

GOAL 3: Good Health and Well-being

GOAL 4: Quality Education

GOAL 5: Gender Equality

GOAL 6: Clean Water and Sanitation

GOAL 7: Affordable and Clean Energy

GOAL 8: Decent Work and Economic Growth

GOAL 9: Industry, Innovation, and Infrastructure

GOAL 10: Reduced Inequality

GOAL 11: Sustainable Cities and Communities

GOAL 12: Responsible Consumption and Production

GOAL 13: Climate Action

GOAL 14: Life Below Water

GOAL 15: Life on Land

GOAL 16: Peace and Justice Strong Institutions

GOAL 17: Partnerships to achieve the Goal

However, despite the many pledges and promises, our progress toward achieving these goals could be better; targets to end hunger and protect climate and biodiversity are entirely off track. Whereas some richer countries are making a degree of progress in the SDGs overall, two-thirds of poorer ones are not expected to meet those that relate even to their most basic needs.

Countries need to be faster to commit to reporting global SDG indicators while replacing SDGs with their proxy indicators, providing no standard benchmark for assessment. Moreover, the local organizations are dormant, while the donations are minimal. According to IISD, "Report after Report by the OECD, Paris21, SDSN, and others show statistics are perennially underfunded, currently attracting a mere 0.34% of total Official Development Assistance (ODA). The funding gap for properly monitoring SDG indicators stands at approximately $200 million annually."

To add to current problems with our progress, the Covid-19 crisis only exacerbated the depth of this challenge; as unemployment increased, so did the working poverty levels while our healthcare system crashed and our economies shattered.

Despite this unfortunate trend, not all is lost. According to the World economics Forum, "the world needs to invest $5-7 trillion per year in sustainable projects to meet the goals –

a far cry from the estimated $3 trillion a year currently being discussed."

According to the World Economics Forum, "Standard Chartered's recent Report, *The $50tn Question*, which surveyed a panel of the world's top 300 investment firms, found that only 13% of the $50 trillion assets they manage is linked to the SDGs. [2] And while two-thirds of their investments are in the developed markets of Europe and North America, just 2, 3, and 5%, respectively, are invested in the Middle East, Africa, and South America.

To address this problem, awareness must be created for investors and firms, urging them to use SDGs as a framework and invest in emerging markets and economies while making. However, people tend to stick with the needs they are familiar with (the US and Europe) while disregarding emerging markets, although they outperform developed markets vastly. It is, therefore, essential that awareness is created, investors are provided adequate data, and governments stimulate SDG-related investments, among many others, such as GRI, SASB, and IRIS

We must consolidate different aspects of our system, utilizing them on a collective front to create a sustainable and prosperous world.

---

2   Standard Chartered. "The $50 Trillion Question." Insights, Standard Chartered, www.sc.com/en/insights/50-trillion-question

Why it Matters

With the dawn of the industrial revolution, humans have depleted 1/3 of the earth's resources as we devoured them. To put it into perspective, if human life existed for 60 mins in a calendar year, we would have managed to deplete 1/3 of our resources in 0.3 seconds. The massive uncontrolled depletion comes with a heavy price as we approach the verge of environmental and financial collapse. In contrast, the wealth of a few grows exponentially and enormously compared to the needs of many. This begs the question, "why has our financial system developed in such a way that the poor lack access to financial tools and services while the rich have greatly depleted our earth's resources?"

Why do we need social finance in the first place? Why hasn't our financial system developed towards benefiting the greater good of both the people and the planet? These questions push the need for a change, for a correction. Social and sustainable finance is the corrective needed to uphold a higher standard of living for all while promoting a cleaner earth.

In the 21st century, while industries are booming like never before and technology is innovating rapidly, we are again on the brink of another recession as diseases run rampant, causing damage despite our finest technologies and solutions. Not to mention the tremendous ecological catastrophes this century has brought, like the European heatwaves and Australian bushfires intensified by the lack of attention to real-world problems. The problem is not the lack of finances or technology. Our greed prevents us from investing in these technologies and solutions that would solve the crisis. Due to our society's capitalistic structure, we have no incentive to invest to avoid something unless it starts harming its industries and markets. Moreover, governments around the world follow this trend, as well as firms.

So, is the world just doomed? Not necessarily. Everybody has a role in addressing the issues of the 21st century. Promoting sustainable finance is going to be our best step moving forward. Citizens can make a huge difference by encouraging congressmen and policymakers to push government funding toward environmental initiatives. Workers can encourage their company to source energy from sustainable sources and work to equip themselves with skills (What kind of skills). Consumers too can make a difference by supporting ethical banks and financial institutions that use their money to support social and sustainable finance objectives. Institution executives can take a variety of actions that fall under the umbrella of sustainable investment: from contributing money to green energy initiatives to improving their businesses such that they uphold ethical ideals like social inclusion or good corporate governance, including having more women on their boards of directors. In simple words, sustainable finance is a mindful way of approaching and taming our capitalistic system. so that contributions to humanity are made, and the needs of the many are prioritized against the wealth and vested interests of a few.

Application and Impact

Global Transition and Impact

As we face an uncertain future, a world plagued with climate change and rampant inequality, we must implement social finance. Although we have realized the catastrophes that await us and are taking steps to change our ways, unfortunately, they are not enough.

As we transition to a greener, more sustainable world, hundreds and perhaps thousands of micro steps must be taken to enable this transition. Firstly, the primary issue being targeted is climate change, involving investment in green technologies, the waning of fossil fuels, and the creation of sustainable infrastructure. The Secondary issue being targeted, which is equally important, is the issue of human life. As we transition to a greener future, we can see the displacement of workers, mass unemployment, marginalization of regions, and the loss of income among the numerous costs humans would bear due to this transition.

While we have successfully recognized the environmental issue that we face, the world still does not notice the costs the vast majority of humans will have to bear as hundreds of thousands and millions are directly or indirectly affected by the activities of these oil companies and the current world order where we majorly use and survive on non-renewables. Therefore, overlooking the human cost while only focusing on the environment sets us on a destructive path of social and economic collapse.

Due to a lack of consensus, uniformity, and terminology, the consideration of human cost is primarily undervalued; capital providers may find it challenging to evaluate the social aspect. For instance, when conducting an ESG analysis, most asset managers concentrate on the 'E' factor when making decisions; however, according to a BNP survey, 51% of respondents said incorporating the social factor into their investment analysis was the most difficult.[3]

Governments, central banks, international organizations, financial service providers, Multilateral Development Banks, international financial institutions, and private financial institutions are just a few of the ecosystem actors crucial to ensuring that capital flows support an equitable transition strategy. The issue of sovereign bonds with just transitional rules attached is one method governments can address. Professor Nick Robins of the Grantham Research Institute believes that sovereign transition bonds would combine the social aspect of transition with the climate initiatives backed by green bonds.

Another option for obtaining the long-term funding needed to reach the objective is through Just Transition Funds. For instance, the European Union established a Just Transition Fund from 2021 to 2027. The fund's primary goals are to support the transition, cut emissions by at least 55% by 2030, and achieve climate neutrality by 2050. The fund includes a social component of environmental

---

[3] BNP Paribas Securities Services. "ESG Global Survey 2021." Securities, BNP Paribas Securities Services, securities.cib.bnpparibas/esg-global-survey-2021.

restoration, worker up- and reskilling, job aid, and inclusive jobseekers' programs to provide employee protection in addition to its goal of supporting economic diversification.

Governments, central banks, and regulators must work together to ensure that the climate transition's socioeconomic effects are prioritized in public finance initiatives. The ILO recommends in its input paper that money from carbon markets and carbon pricing be used to pay for programs that would address the social and employment effects of decarbonization. Another example of such a policy is fostering a transparent regulatory framework for the socioeconomic effects of climate transition initiatives. In order to incorporate the social dimension of transition methods, this entails establishing relevant disclosures, standards, and accountability metrics.

Diversity, Equity, and Inclusion Investing

Integrating diversity, equity, and inclusion (DEI) factors into investments from the public and private sectors entail a complex framework. In simple terms, such an effort would include a commitment of an entity's capital to diverse leadership and governance and to have these attributes within the respective workforce. Such a structure ultimately aims to create positive and equitable change while creating competitive returns, which frequently tend to be a byproduct.

For some figures to grasp the drivers or the compelling nature of DEI investments, in both a financial and moral sense, a study by the Knight Foundation regarding the endowments of the wealthiest US colleges and universities reports the following:[4]

- 29.4% of women-owned private equity firms perform in the top quartile.

- 34.1% of private equity firms that are owned by historically underrepresented minorities perform in the top quartile.

---

4   "Few of the Nation's Wealthiest Universities Share Data for Knight-NYU Stern Center Study of Asset Manager Diversity in Higher Ed." Knight Foundation, July 15, 2021. https://knightfoundation.org/press/releases/few-of-the-nations-wealthiest-universities-share-data-for-knight-nyu-stern-center-study-of-asset-manager-diversity-in-higher-ed/

- Companies with solid diversity performed 19% better than their average counterparts in terms of innovation revenues.

- Outstanding racial and ethnic diversity led to a 35% boost, and remarkable gender diversity led to a 19% boost compared to the firm's more homogeneous counterparts.

In essence, consideration and prioritization of DEI strategies and practices can improve the performance of the workforce and, in turn, improve the firm's routines and thus benefit stakeholders. The reason for such a positive correlation is tied to the role of DEI in various settings—or the workspace in this case. The consequential nature of DEI factors surpasses programs, policies, and training modules within a firm: on a more intimate level, diverse, inclusive, and equitable firms spur the sharing of different, unique sentiments, beliefs, and perceptions, thus establishing values of respect, open-mindedness, and compassion as a necessity for functional behavior.

Such interactions and exposures, even at the executive level, generally translate to financial performance, hence the link between social finance and DEI factors. According to a study by McKinsey & Company, gender and ethnic diversity correlates to profitability and performance.[5] This is due to components such as the level of attraction to

---

5   "Diversity Wins: How Inclusion Matters." McKinsey & Company, 2021.https://www.mckinsey.com/featured-insights/diversity-and-inclusion/diversity-wins-how-inclusion-matters

prospective talent, satisfaction from the public and the workforce, and the decision-making process in areas of varying significance.

There are many guides and measures to the end; an employer's seeking to foster and prioritize DEI factors, however, an investor's considerations are naturally different. Experts highlight that an investor must not only distinguish among the terms comprising DEI per se but also the broader implications of DEI on investments. For one, Anne E. Robinson, general counsel of Vanguard, states that DEI risks are potentially equally significant and disruptive as the better-known climate-related risks.[6] She elaborates that although DEI falls are typically placed under the governance factor of ESG, they can extend even to environmental factors.

In the end, despite the increasing popularity and awareness of DEI investing and its potency, the SEC found that not even 1% of the $70 trillion in industrial assets are women or minority-managed. The potential of this aspect of social finance has yet to be realized as of this writing, neither inequitable nor economic respect. As with most things, further research and time will highlight the actual value of DEI in investment.

---

6 "Investors Are Waking Up to the Market Potential of Diversity, Equity and Inclusion." Forbes, https://www.forbes.com/sites/bonniechiu/2022/03/01/investors-are-waking-up-to-market

Impact Bonds: Communities and Poverty Alleviation

One of the essential instruments through which social finance can fund the delivery of public services is the impact bond. It started in the UK in 2010, when Prime Minister Gordon Brown strove to pilot this tool as a means to tackling problems in society like homelessness and unemployment. New ideas could be explored with support from impact bonds for complex issues requiring complex solutions. What exactly is an impact bond? Simply put, it's a financial partnership between an investor and an outcome-payer where payments are made upon the completion of a service or effort, usually seen through by a service provider. For a proper, nuanced definition, the GO Lab states, "impact bonds are outcome-based contracts that incorporate the use of private funding from investors to cover the upfront capital required for a provider to set up and deliver a service."

There are many terms and nuances concerning impact bonds, but the two significant types are frequently known as social impact bonds (SIBs) and development impact bonds (DIBs). Although both focus on social outcomes in a particular area, the outcome-payer for SIBs is usually a domestic government, and for DIBs, it's usually one or more donors—foreign, household, or both.

In terms of the investment itself, the risks associated with impact bonds tend to differ from those of regular bonds. The main risk is that the investment depends on the success of a particular social outcome while also incurring default and inflation risks. Naturally, it's also more work to manage and make such an investment due to the generally small amount of complex data. In practice, such aspects have led to funding being excluded from the public sector, albeit both private and public sectors hold the ability. It's also very difficult to casually associate the investment, financed with the bond, with the observed social outcome. Nevertheless, impact investing has been growing in popularity. If it wasn't clear already, providing investment to address social and environmental issues allows individuals and companies to give back to communities and become more socially responsible.

One example of impact investing working to alleviate poverty-related issues is the Cameroon Kangaroo Mother Care (KMC), a DIB launched in 2018 by governmental and international organizations devoted to poverty and public health. The program strove to reduce infant morbidity and mortality in Cameroon's five poor regions. The funding provided support, training, and equipment to clinicians in those communities and hospitals. Such an effort was crucial and consequential: according to Social Finance US (a non-profit), "almost one in two low-birth-weight and preterm infants dies after birth in Cameroon."

Similarly, another DIB sought to bring safe sanitation to rural Cambodian communities to reduce and eradicate the formerly high rates of open defecation. The $10 million impact bond addressed the central issue of poor sanitation, which can cause severe health-related and social problems.

What distinguishes the approach of this DIB from the previous example is that it's not precisely input-based aid. Instead, it funds a broader sanitation marketing program that meets local demand and generates jobs to sustain markets. This conception is essential since impact bonds don't last forever.

Ultimately, impact bonds, a social finance instrument, can potentially unite expertise and solutions, encourage and allow unique ideas and approaches, and bolster voluntary efforts. It's important to acknowledge the limitations of impact bonds as well, however, particularly in the context of communities and poverty alleviation. Their feasibility depends on quantifiability, outcome-measurement potential, and timing concerning community issues. There may be financial and outcome-definition-related concerns as well. The most relevant obstacle, though, is from the ideological standpoint: the morality of seeking profit out of impactful strategies in impuissant communities. Regardless of its limitations, impact bonds have and will continue to serve as a component of the social finance toolbox/repertoire, primarily as the need arises and honing continues.

Microfinance

We must uplift millions on the verge of collapse, those more than 820 million experiencing starvation, those 2 billion people who don't have access to clean drinking water, and those 72 million children who remain unschooled. Furthermore, the other millions in underdeveloped and developing countries are most vulnerable to climate change and industrial activities due to a lack of investment, infrastructure, and funds. We must address these issues to create a truly sustainable world for all.

Microfinance is one way to uplift low-income individuals and, at the very least, sustain them. Investopedia says, "Microfinance, also called microcredit, is a banking service provided to unemployed or low-income individuals or groups who otherwise would have no other access to financial services."

These microfinance services in low-income countries differ from those in well-developed countries. We have observed that microfinance initiatives in impoverished nations such as Bangladesh, where there were over 20 million micro borrowers, can be key in lifting millions out of poverty. These services are not restricted to just financial support, but also various other activities such as seminars that help stimulate enterprise. However, microfinance has taken up a different form in developed nations, where microfinance is just synonymous with just small loans and nothing more.

These microfinance initiatives, similar to those in other underdeveloped nations, must be emulated in other areas because many people who live on less than **$2 a day may** attempt to spend, save and borrow. However, it is simply not feasible for them on such a meager amount. They may require more money to survive, so they may look up to family and friends for money and sometimes even loan sharks. Making the lives of such families and individuals smoother, more accessible, and better, microfinance is a great way to help them.

Microfinance allows people to take small loans, ranging from $100 to as large as $25000, in a legally abiding manner and consistent with lending practices. Microfinance also seeks to help businesses and foster entrepreneurship in these unprivileged communities, providing a wide range of support. According to Investopedia, "support a large number of activities that range from providing the basics—like bank checking and savings accounts—to startup capital for small business entrepreneurs and educational programs that teach the principles of investing. These programs can focus on such skills as bookkeeping, cash-flow management, and technical or professional skills, like accounting."

Unlike typical banking situations where individuals are supposed to have collateral to borrow, microfinance organizations want to see entrepreneurs succeed and instead have an introductory money management course, after which they may proceed for a loan under the guidance of a loan officer.

The existence of such facilities, especially in impoverished countries such as Uganda, has benefited more than 500 million people directly or indirectly, according to the World Bank. As of 2021, more than 120 million people helped now. However, these operations are only available to the minority, while over 1.7 billion poor don't have access to basic financial accounts.

Microfinance initiatives have been unsuccessful thus far. The difficulty comes in determining the risk of providing loans to impoverished people who don't have a credit score or other means of proving trustability. But, that doesn't mean it's impossible. Companies like Nuru work in the Dominican Republic of Congo. They work to install energy infrastructures like solar power to provide the population with financial services on the internet. Microfinance can have a significant impact on society, aiding millions and creating countless heartwarming stories as they help entrepreneurs kick-start their businesses, create jobs capital, and positively impact the community. Taking this forward can only affect more people, the 1.7 billion people who still have to endure harsh conditions and create a sustainable and thriving world for all.

Crowdfunding and Angel Investing

Crowdfunding and Angel Investing offer a unique opportunity where investors can fund a world-changing initiative while turning a profit. Crowdfunding is when a company collects funds through investments, loans, or donations to meet a financial requirement to follow through with a plan. These funds can come from a variety of sources both private and public. Syncany Diagrams demonstrate the flow of capital to its impact. This differs from Angel Investing, where money received from investors is strictly provided as an investment, in the hopes of profit. Angel investors usually come from a venture capital firm, an investment fund that invests in startups.

In Social Enterprise funding, investors are motivated by monetary, social, and environmental returns. Typically, investors are promised a benefit to society or the environment from their actions with money. Before, investors were more motivated to invest in a project when: they had a sound business model, a solid financial plan, were trustworthy, and had a passion for their project. Investors can find initiatives in many various ways. Some include word of mouth, direct contact from a business representative, or startup platforms. Some reputable startup platforms include:

- Propel(x)[7] is a fundraising platform focused on technology companies in the energy, food, agriculture, and financial technologies sectors. They have raised over **2 billion dollars** for a multitude of various startups.

7 Propel(x), https://www.propelx.com.

They have had startups who work in enterprise blockchain, infectious disease prevention, and more.

- UpEffect[8] is a fundraising platform focused on social innovators. They have worked to raise money for the war in Ukraine, women's rights, fresh drinking water, and more. UpEffect raised $45,000 for water filtration systems in impoverished parts of Bali, Indonesia. Additionally, they raised $15,000 for comprehensive primary health care in Thane, India.

An additional way social enterprises can acquire funding is through donations or competition rewards. There are many competitions that some social enterprises can fall under.

- The MIT SOLV[ED][9] Youth Innovation Challenge is aimed at under 24 years old problem solvers looking to change the world using technology.

- The VELA Education Fund[10] is a grant program for entrepreneurs looking to improve education around the world.

Both profit businesses and non-profits can seek funding. Still today, there needs to be more funding for social enterprises. Whether due to political affiliation or distrust in the companies, people continue to decline social finance initiatives. This poses a severe problem because social enterprises are created based on social, economic, and environmental change. Change is necessary to aid our world.

8 UpEffect, https://www.theupeffect.com.
9 MIT Solve. https://solve.mit.edu/
10 Vela Education Fund, https://velaedfund.org/

Green Finance and Environmental Impact

With the dawn of the industrial revolution, humans have depleted 1/3 of the earth's resources as we devoured them. To put it into perspective, if human life existed for 37 mins in a calendar year, we would have managed to deplete 1/3 of our resources in 0.2 seconds. The massive uncontrolled depletion comes with a heavy price to pay as we approach the verge of environmental and financial collapse. In contrast, the wealth of a few grows exponentially and enormously compared to the needs of many.

In the 21st century, while industries are booming like never before and technology is at its finest, we are again on the brink of a recession. At the same time, diseases run rampant, and millions starve. Not to mention the tremendous ecological catastrophes this century has brought, from the European heatwaves and Australian bushfires to the deforestation of the Amazon rainforests and the melting of polar ice caps. We see massive environmental cataclysms, yet little to no efforts to solve these problems compared to their magnitude and urgency—the United Nations issued code red for humanity under their new IPCC report. If we don't halve our carbon emissions by 2030, all may very well be lost as temperatures soar and countries experience adverse floodings, droughts, heatwaves, and even more extreme weather phenomena.

We must invest in green technologies, infrastructure, and policies to achieve our net-zero goals before it is too late. Businesses and firms must play a considerable role by committing to environmental consciousness and CSR through green investing.

Investopedia says, "Green investing seeks to support business practices that have a favorable impact on the natural environment. Often grouped with socially responsible investing (SRI) or environmental, social, and governance (ESG) criteria, green investments focus on companies or projects committed to the conservation of natural resources, pollution reduction, or other environmentally conscious business practices."

We must hold firms accountable for their practices by introducing government regulations and incentives for green investing to create a sustainable world.

We can see these practices already taking place in Europe, where European Commission commissioners Thierry Breton and Didier Reynders submitted the idea for a Directive on Corporate Sustainability Due Diligence, which would require businesses to recognize, stop, and mitigate human rights and environmental abuses along their value chain. The Directive will be applicable to EU businesses with 500 or more employees and a net global turnover of more than €150 million.

These steps are likely to significantly alter the ways businesses operate and should set an example of regulation to hold businesses accountable.

Case Studies

Women's World Banking

For over 40 years, the non-profit organization known as Women's World Banking (WWB) has led the way to the empowerment of low-income women through financial tools—to achieve financial inclusion. WWB achieves this "through a combination of [their] cutting-edge research; policy and advocacy engagement; scalable, market-driven digital financial solutions; gender lens private equity fund; and leadership and diversity programs." In other words, they strive to open up financial, informational, and market-related access to extend economic involvement to this demographic.

From a more precise standpoint, WWB takes intricate measures through its global network of 62 financial institutions across 35 markets: creating new credit, savings, and insurance products to build financial cushions and spur the transition from microfinance. What sets WWB apart is both its mission and its personalized research approach, where they devise financially sustainable solutions while understanding and meeting needs. In terms of the underlying components of the process, the main focus of their expertise lies in four areas: research and perspectives, products and solutions, leadership and diversity, and gender lens investing.

One example of work in the first and second areas is tied to collateral, an asset that can be seized under a failure of loan repayment. Specifically, a movable attribute to collateral benefits women more than men since they are less likely to possess fixed assets. Women are also less likely to access credit and other financial tools and services. Movable collateral is equitable and valuable in allowing and facilitating women's leveraging capital, which can provide economic, commercial, and personal benefits. WWB comes in to positively utilize this tool by advocating for the creation of portable collateral systems. The three case studies on their website highlight their work and the impact of such systems in Colombia, Ghana, and Laos. In essence, these systems offer both the framework and capacity needed to serve debtors and creditors and ensure transparency and legal redress mechanisms. In brief, they show the great potential for increasing credit to enterprises of various sizes and contrast the low-impact of these systems in other markets, which most likely faced challenges such as a lack of revenue.

A second example that demonstrates the third and fourth areas can be explored through WWB Capital Banking Partners, LP. This fund is a private equity limited partnership that directly invests in institutions focusing on women. This is a more explicit example of social finance at play in the real world in that investors are, in effect, investing in the leadership and growth of women by influencing institutions to include and involve women in their various functions. The gender lens investing at play here contributes to leadership and diversity and financial outperformance, which is influenced in part by the DEI contribution (if this wasn't made clear already from reading the chapter on DEI).

In the end, the impact achieved through WWB goes beyond the numbers. The tens of millions of dollars of investments, millions of clients, and high percentages of outperformance only quantify the impact achieved at the core: paving the way to economic empowerment for an underprivileged group—an example of a core element of social finance.

Ecology Building Society

The green movement of the late 1970s did more than shine light on environmental destruction: it sparked the growth and the beginnings of the Ecology Building Society. This group sought the most significant degree of environmental sustainability.

For some context, the movement began in the 1960s due to conservationist and preservationist ideologies in the post-World War II era or, in particular, due to the post-World War II economy and its environmental implications. The movement created political pressure and attention regarding air and water pollution. By the late 1970s and beyond, it broadened its focus to address the effects of toxic waste disposal and global warming. A more subtle emphasis of the movement was simple living and self-sufficiency, which is where Ecology came in.

Ecology emerged due to the difficulty among environmentalists in financing environmental building renovations and sustainable development. The renovations of older properties led to the incurrence of expensive bridge loans, contractors, and additional work. Ecology's establishment in 1981 aspired to facilitate such projects through lending, though they committed to ethical principles and their mission of promoting sustainable communities and environmental protection.

Today, Ecology has risen far above the £5,000 capital it held in 1981 to fund its pursuits. In 2020 alone, Ecology lent over **£39.3 million** to 240 projects and properties that have taken sustainable measures. These numbers highlight more than society's success, especially the growth they convey.

Ecology's success demonstrates the need for such environmental and infrastructure-related social finance instruments. Their experience and acumen in lending for particular markets also pose a critical issue. In this case, restricted markets usually translate to people who might be ineligible for loans without Ecology. As a result, value and growth may not always be the primary pursuit, and funding for initiating ESG-related projects may only sometimes be guaranteed. Nevertheless, their relatively small size from a financial and corporate standpoint doesn't obscure the impact they've achieved in an environmental, social, and ethical sense.

Triodos Bank: Netherland's First Social Bank

Triodos Bank, created by Esteban Barosso in late 1988 because he understood the importance of the emerging social finance sector, is the first social bank in the Netherlands. Unlike a typical bank, which uses funds to promote profitability through loans, social banks (sometimes called ethics banks) use funds to promote social, environmental, and cultural change. However, like a typical bank, social banks still provide a place to hold money for individuals and businesses and provide loans. They pride themselves in their sustainable initiatives, only servicing companies that promote sustainability.

They're very transparent about using individuals' and companies' funds to promote social, environmental, and cultural change. The British Financial Times named Triodos Bank "The Most Sustainable Bank of the Year". To date, the bank has funded over 5000 projects in 47 countries. Some of their projects include

- The creation of solar farms through ECOOO in Madrid, Spain T

- The spread of organic seafood around Belgium and France with Food4Good.

- Using bee products like pollen and honey to create therapeutic and food products in the Canary Islands through the company Epitek.

- Creating sustainable workplaces in up-and-coming creative districts for play theaters, music venues, and more in London, England.

While most of their change is environmental change, they enact changes in microfinance, community projects, healthcare, and many more.

Balancing profitability, change, and risk is a hurdle for all social banks. Social Banks need to guarantee minimal risk and not lose people's money and fall into bankruptcy. Luckily, Triodos has been very successful through its many ventures.

The future goals of Triodos only help to improve its sustainability goals. They wish to have Net-Zero greenhouse gas emissions by 2035 through their bank and the ventures they fund.

Accion Micro-Credit

Accion (Americans for Community Cooperation in Other Nations) is a non-profit established in 1961 that works to empower underserved nations with financial services. Backed by Citigroup, Mastercard, Credit Suisse, and FMO, they work on every continent except Antarctica. Accion helps individuals, families, small businesses, and communities improve their financial situation.

Many struggle to make ends meet with their income. In Brazil, where an operation is set up, wages can be as little as 200 USD per month. This needs to leave more for housing, food, child care, and other necessary expenses. Accion works to create and find jobs for individuals to increase their household income, so they're able to cover these essential expenses. They also provide loans to help kickstart small businesses and people's finances. Through their partners, they can provide loans at forgiving interest rates.

Using microfinance, they are given access to financial services that help them improve their situation. Whether making investments, creating better budgets, or using other tools, they can make quick changes to their finances. Accion connects people to microfinance enterprises which aids them in these efforts.

Most importantly, they work to ensure these effects are sustainable and last for the future. After all, it isn't beneficial if the results are temporary and minimal. People need long-lasting financial prosperity. With Accion, they are given the support and ability to improve their financial position for the long term.

They have dispersed over **$500 million** through 600,000+ loans for Latin America alone. They are still working tirelessly to improve the global financial situation of the masses.

The Future Ahead

Social Entrepreneurship and Bank

Social Entrepreneurship is when entrepreneurs create a startup that directly addresses social issues, some of which include climate change, food and water access, and inequality. Bill Drayton, a Harvard graduate, pioneered the phrase "Social Entrepreneur" in 1980 with his creation of the business Ashoka.

Ashoka works to promote social entrepreneurship. They partner with organizations to create large-scale change around the world. Their numerous fellows, and the people they work with, have made significant changes in all areas.

- Brittany Young with B360 encourages youth minority dirt bikers in Baltimore, Maryland, to pursue an interest in STEM (Science, Technology, Engineering, and Math) and help them fight inequality.

- Heber Brown III connects black churches to help food insecurity in the black community.

- Daquan Oliver promotes youth entrepreneurship in underserved school districts.

More than just Ashoka and their fellows exist. Shiza Shadid worked to create the Malala Fund. She is the mentor of Malala Yousafzai, the youngest-ever Nobel prize winner. The Malala Fund makes excellent and safe education for young women in Pakistan.

Social banks or sustainable banks are similar to social entrepreneurship because they both work to promote social change. Social banks promote change by connecting people, sustainable investing, and social lending.

Banks are not just a place to store and invest your money. They are also a place to talk with experts about managing your money. Some social banks work to make connecting with finance experts easier. Using social media and new platforms, they connect you with experts where you can discuss how to invest your money, spend your money, stay sustainable, and any other finance questions you may have.

Banks, specifically wealth management-focused banks, can help you invest in more sustainable companies. Companies that don't emit large amounts of greenhouse gasses use unethical business methods. Companies committing these acts are riskier and less favorable to the community because people don't trust them as much.

Social lending took off after the 2008 financial crisis when people could not obtain loans because banks didn't offer them. Social lending provides a way for people to get loans without the risks of big banks denying them, exploiting them, and other dangers.

Private and Public Sector

Due to the ever-increasing quantities and better quality of social finance/ESG data, impact investing is increasing in popularity and plausibility. The recent evidence of successful exits in social finance investments reflects honing acumen and expertise, new, varied products, and utilization of new markets and clients in the impact-backed investment world.

As demand for social finance products and services rises (mostly in emerging economies), the result will be more regulation and a degree of oversight. As both correlation and causation, with further application of data and metrics regarding ESG factors and impact measurement and management, there will likely be a surge in impact-driven investors seeking to create change in their desired areas and retail investors seeking long-term returns.

In terms of more specific implications for the public and private sectors, available funding and goals/commitments will likely drive spending while serving the government/corporation's constituents in the best way possible. More organizations and groups are pushing and aiding governments in improving social service delivery systems in the public sector. According to Social Finance US, "strengthening evidence-oriented policy analysis, designing implementation plans, developing outcomes-focused funding tools, and establishing governance committees" are all components of the road ahead for the non-profit and public sectors. From a governmental standpoint, the state's role in building and shaping social finance markets through public policy will also be a significant component since the emerging toolbox will significantly shape the social finance world.

Of course, the overall impact and cooperation in the road ahead will also depend heavily on the private sector. Leveraging private capital to address global and local challenges and goals is a core mission of social finance. Particularly for the private sector, there will be challenges and potential in the road ahead. Both outcomes will depend on the competitiveness of returns, startup, and regulatory costs, access to various investors, and mainstream banking. Nonetheless, the momentum sparked by large asset holders in the private sector integrating purpose and impact indicates that the road ahead might comprise the mainstreaming of social finance.

As exciting as the prospects for mainstreaming and an increase in capital, talent, and research in the social finance landscape seem, both rhetoric and levels of skepticism around quality, in a service and product-related sense, will influence the future of social finance. Of course, healthy skepticism and the increasing involvement of united thinkers and leaders in both sectors will only enhance and magnify the impact and functionality of this field.

Current and Future Challenges

Although Social Finance has come a long way, making significant changes, it has much to improve upon.

The absence of industry standards is one of the current issues plaguing social finance. Since there is no universally accepted definition of "social finance," it is challenging for organizations to effectively communicate their impact to stakeholders and for investors to evaluate the social impact of their investments.

Another contemporary issue is the lack of accurate data and measures for assessing the social impact of investments. Due to this, it is challenging for organizations to explain their impact to potential investors and for investors to evaluate the success of their investments.

Regulation is a persistent issue in the field of social finance as there are frequently ambiguous norms and guidelines for impact investing. This makes it challenging for organizations to negotiate the legal and regulatory environment and reduces the amount of capital accessible for impact investments.

There is currently no accepted standard for impact assessment, which presents another difficulty in measuring and accounting for social impact. To attract investments, organizations must be able to assess and communicate their impact, but doing so can be challenging without the right frameworks and tools.

The possibility for "greenwashing" or "impact washing" in social finance represents a future challenge. There is a chance that some organizations could make claims about having a positive social or environmental impact without actually achieving it as the demand for socially responsible investments rises. Due to this, investors may become confused and distrustful, and the sector of social finance as a whole may lose credibility.

The difficulty of scaling up to fulfill the rising demand for impact investments is a major challenge facing the field of social finance. There is a demand for additional impact investment options that can handle huge pools of wealth as more and more investors try to match their investments with their values. It will be necessary to do this by developing new financial tools and impact investing opportunities. In order to manage and expand the potential for impact investments, it is also necessary to have a team that has received the right training and has knowledge and skills in the field of social finance.

Overall, despite recent major advancements in the subject of social finance, there are still numerous obstacles to be overcome. It will be crucial to address these issues in order for social finance to develop and realize its full potential. This includes standardizing the industry, enhancing data and metrics, preventing "greenwashing" and "impact washing," scaling up impact investment opportunities and having a properly educated workforce.

Cryptocurrency and Blockchain

Advances in financial technology pave the way for new methods to push social finance initiatives. While Bitcoin, Ethereum, and "meme coins" like DogeCoin or Shiba Inu dominate the media, they aren't the type of cryptocurrency we're talking about. These coins promote the opposite of what social finance initiatives seek to improve, they cause environmental destruction. This is because these coins support cryptocurrency mining, the verifying of transactions on a blockchain through the usage of computer power in return for cryptocurrency payment. People and companies build large mining farms in order to maximize the amount they can earn. These large mining farms lead to intense environmental issues because of the large amounts of typically unethically sourced power the cryptocurrency miners rely on. Additionally, because of the anonymous nature of cryptocurrency being such that transactions cant be tracked, it can be used in illegal activities. Secretary of the Treasury, Janet Yellen, said, "I think many (cryptocurrencies) are used, at least in a transaction sense, mainly for illicit financing."[11]

However, this isn't to say that all cryptocurrency and blockchain efforts are anti-environment. Blockchain offers many features that benefit its use in social and environmental initiatives. Blockchain offers a decentralized network,

---

[11] Lennon, Hailey. "The False Narrative Of Bitcoin's Role In Illicit Activity." Forbes, 2 August 2018, https://www.forbes.com/sites/haileylennon/2021/01/19/the-false-narrative-of-bitcoins-role-in-illicit-activity/?sh=f1893803432f.

not controlled by a government or company, so it has unlimited possibilities because it doesn't have to meet any certain regulations. This is optimal because, for initiatives in countries with political instability, there isn't additional difficulty implementing themselves. Additionally, this allows it to be used worldwide anywhere by anybody that has internet access because it doesn't have to meet individual country's regulations. This is especially important for social and environmental initiatives that take place in underserved communities. Initiatives can set up an internet connection, if one does not currently exist, and harness the power of blockchain.

But how can blockchain be used to promote good? Impact Tokens are digital tokens or cryptocurrencies whose purpose is to support projects with social and/or environmental impact.

- Plastic Bank[12] uses blockchain to collect and trade plastic waste items for essential items in impoverished areas.

- Veridium[13] uses digital tokens to track a company's carbon output and offset the process in its supply chain.

- Moeda[14] is a social investment platform that lets investors fund microloans for underserved women entrepreneurs in Brazil.

---

12 Plastic Bank, https://plasticbank.com/
13 Veridium, https://www.veridium.io/
14 Moeda, https://moeda.finance/

- SolarCoin[15] incentivizes the creation of solar energy by helping initiatives fund themselves through their cryptocurrency.

As blockchain and cryptocurrency technology develop even more, social and environmental problems can be solved.

---

15   Solar Coin, https://solarcoin.org/

Getting Involved

Personal Finance

How can you make your personal finance more sustainable? Why would you want to make your finances more sustainable? Everything you choose, like your bank, credit cards, utilities, and investments, can be more sustainable.

There are many ways to make your baking more sustainable. It would be best if you didn't use banks that aren't environmentally friendly. Some banks use your money to enable gas, oil, and coal extraction. But, many banks make ecologically responsible decisions. They use your money to fund future initiatives, green energy, and a cleaner planet. Websites like bank. green[16], for example, rate banks based on their sustainability. You can use the ratings to make a decision better. Just because you're using a sustainable bank does not mean you're missing out on services other banks offer. You can still access ATMs, checking accounts, saving accounts, loans, FDIC protection, and more.

Additionally, you can apply for environmentally friendly credit and debit cards. Some cards are made from recyclable materials like wood, plastics, and metals. An example is the Tree Card[17], made from wood, which plants a tree for every $50 you spend. Another card, the Beneficial State Bank Card[18], supports climate change-related non-profits.

---

16 Bank.Green, https://bank.green/.
17 Tree Card, https://ecosia.treecard.org/
18 Beneficial State Bank, https://www.beneficialstatebank.com/

Also, you can swap your utilities for more sustainable options. Investing in solar panels can help the environment by not using fossil fuels for energy and save you money in the long run. Another great option is using sustainable phone services like CREDO Mobile[19]. They promote different non-profits like environmental causes and social causes.

Even your investments can be more environmentally friendly. You can invest in socially responsible funds like VFTAX (Vanguard FTSE Social Index Fund). Impact bonds and SRI are great options too.

The field is rapidly developing, with new companies starting every day. This list is just a few of the current ways. Don't limit yourself to these. There are many ways to make your finances more sustainable and improve your future impact.

---

19   Credo Mobile, https://www.credomobile.com/

Careers

Because the popularity, as well as the practice and consideration of social finance components, is increasing, the demand for employees, expertise, and research in this field are growing accordingly. Both the materiality and significance of ESG factors in impact investing, for example, have led to openings in corporations and organizations for professionals working to related ends.

Regarding impact investing, the titles of ESG analyst and sustainability consultant are very pertinent. An ESG analyst conducts research and analysis on ESG factors and disclosures. In other words, they perform due diligence through a social finance lens before offering financial advice based on their respective tasks and research. On the other hand, a sustainability consultant may work with multiple firms to determine, from a sustainability standpoint, whether to proceed with a project. Generally, both positions involve measuring potential impact and materiality and providing advice for more efficient, considerate, and financially sound measures.

There are also broader roles involved in the impact investing world, naturally. Impact investments are investments, and thus the role of financial advisors and researchers is vital. In this context, a financial advisor (or consultant) would evaluate potential returns, risk factors, and market trends to determine the profitability of investments while also maximizing positive impact. Researchers, however, tend to take the first steps since they search for sustainable and impactful investing opportunities and study their feasibility and value.

On a slightly different note, the field of social finance has many intersections and constituents in areas such as developmental, environmental, and health economics, to name a few. These fields answer essential questions to the corporate world: to what extent will businesses, organizations, governments, and investors consider developmental, environmental, and health responsibilities and consequences from an economic and numerical standpoint? As regulations, goals, and awareness have increased in these areas, many employment opportunities for economists and analysts have also sprung up.

Alternatively, many governmental roles can aid the success of social finance initiatives. Especially now, we need congressmen and cabinet staff to push climate initiative policies.

As exciting and fulfilling as some of these careers may seem, their natural beauty lies in the underlying goals and the global movement toward meeting SDGs, new organizational and governmental regulations, and ESG-related considerations, which collectively play a significant role in creating a sustainable and socially responsible world.

Institutions and Enterprises

In 1840, the idea behind social enterprises was conceived in Europe. It offered a new take on creating a company whose business plan is centered around environmental and social change rather than focusing on profitability. The businesses still don't make a profit and offer free products. It means they use funds to help stimulate change.

Anything from banks, travel companies, and eyeglass retailers can become social enterprises. This means the structure of social enterprises can greatly vary from a non-profit structure, LLC, or other.

Grameen Bank[20] is a social enterprise in rural Bangladesh. As a country in the top 50 most impoverished in the world according to the world population review, 20% of its population is below the poverty line. Grameen Bank offers loans without the need for collateral. Instead, they have a banking system based on trust. The bank was started on the idea that if you give impoverished humans access to financial tools and services, they can repair their situation and create world change.

Additionally, I to We[21] is a company that provides valuable travel experiences for everyone. The travels help show people different cultures and let them experience how other people live first-hand. All the joys and difficult times people from other countries go through. They also offer a Track

---

20 Grameen Bank. https://www.grameenbank.org.
21 I to We, https://www.we.org.

Your Impact platform. This allows participants to support social change through spending, like providing lunches and fresh water for impoverished children in Kenya.

Also, Warby Parker,[22] a well-established eyeglasses retailer, is a social enterprise. For every pair of glasses they sell, they donate a pair to someone in need in a developing country. They estimate that they have donated more than 1 million pairs, according to Entrepreneur Magazine. The buy-a-pair, give-a-pair model has significantly impacted in-need people around the globe and returned a profit for the glasses maker.

While there are many social enterprises, change is always in need. The world will constantly change as the social finance sector emerges more and more.

---

22 Warby Parker, https://www.warbyparker.com.

Taking Initiative

Every new field, discovery, service, product, organization, etc., is naturally the result of an initiative by an individual or group. For us at Financitive, it was the enthusiasm within all three of us founders and the desire to use our enthusiasm for the greater good that led to the creation of our organization. Even the idea for our initiative wouldn't have been possible, in fact, if it weren't for the numerous social finance research and initiatives before us and the effort put into all individual components.

What's unique about a social finance initiative, from our experience, is the idea of building something new based on a relatively new world. In other older and well-explored areas of study, enough research and experience have led to numerous pre-existing opportunities, projects, and corporations to get involved in and build off, even for students. Pure finance and business, for example, exemplify this notion very well: from clubs like a school investment club to organizations like DECA to even programs and apps for teen investing and startups. Of course, initiatives in these more established areas should not be disparaged. But the fact is that the process is greatly facilitated and more navigable.

With a social finance initiative, on the contrary, luck and determination are also factors, in addition to intrinsic hard work and creativity. At Financitive, even our discovery of the social finance world was lucky, and any initiative or project under our organization required lengthy discussions, determination, and creativity. For any initiative, though, a flexible guiding theme or goal that doesn't include much detail will help immensely, regardless of difficulty and practicality. For us, it was the mission to educate and achieve impact through new ways in a relatively new field that served as guidance. The flexibility of this mission enabled us to persevere and accomplish despite external setbacks.

We hope this book has offered more than a glimpse into the beautiful, potent world of social finance. We hope it has instilled the insight that new fields, ideas, and notions are worth questioning and embracing. In other words, everything is worth exploring to a degree or without bounds, depending on your passion and vision. After all, such self-driven exposures are what ultimately lead to innovation and initiative in areas that have the potential to solve significant problems in our world.

For further readings, which were useful to our own research as well, we highly recommend *The Essentials of Social Finance* by Andreas Andrikopoulos, *The Socioeconomic Theory of Finance* by Robert Prechter, *Demystifying Social Finance and Social Investment* by Mark Salway and Paul Palmer, *Doughnut Economics: Seven Ways to Think Like a 21st-Century Economist* by Kate Raworth, and *Sustainable: Moving Beyond ESG to Impact Investing* by Terrence Keeley.

Authors' Note

As high school students participating in clubs and teams, taking coursework and assessments, and running an organization, writing this book has been both difficult and incredibly rewarding. For one, we were able to gain skills that extended beyond learning and management: skills that could make a tangible impact on what's available in the educational ecosystem. In addition, through ideation, research, and partnerships, we met and formed strong relationships with organizations, professionals, and academics.

Needless to say, this book would not have been possible without the people we worked with. First, we would like to thank our friends, families, and teachers for their support and enthusiasm throughout this process. From financial to moral support, their love and compassion motivated us to make progress and develop new relationships as well.

In addition, we want to thank Prof. Andreas Andrikopoulos and Prof. Jason Jay for mentoring our research and reviewing our book but, most of all, for their support and encouragement for our mission. While teaching, leading, and conducting research at their own institutions, the University of Piraeus and Massachusetts Institute of Technology, respectively, they replied to our emails and were more than happy to be interviewed. Prof. Mark Kramer too was interviewed, and provided profound insights that extended far beyond social finance itself and into what it means to find meaning in society and personal endeavors. We are grateful for and inspired by their truly exemplifying what it means to be a great educator.

Of course, our own interests in creating change and being civic innovators was a result of the students and leaders of the Civics Unplugged program. Each and every member of this fellowship impacted us in many ways, but, in particular, we want to express our gratitude and appreciation toward Thanasi Dilos, Josh Thompson, and Nick Delis for supporting our organization, Financitive, and for the invaluable advice, kindness, and resources they offered and continue to offer—not only to us, but thousands of young civic leaders around the world.

Lastly, we want to thank members of Bumper Investing, a fintech startup that not only equipped us with free financial knowledge and resources through their ambassador program but also continued to advise and reach out regarding our work even afterward. Harrison Martindale taught us more than the fundamentals of finance, for his advice and willingness to talk to us showed us what it meant to be a leader in the financial space and beyond. We are extremely thankful for the people who have played a significant role in our lives and helped realize our resources for countless others. At Financitive, though, our work has only begun, and we are very excited about our future projects and initiatives.

Glossary

3 R's Reduce, Reuse, Recycle is a slogan for the practice of reducing product waste by recycling or reusing it for another product.

Biodegradable A product that reduces environmental waste by disintegrating after being discarded. In particular, products that can be broken down into innocuous products by the action of living organisms.

Blended Value The evaluation of businesses, non-profits, and investments based on their environment, financial, and social value. This emerging framework is calculated, essentially, by the value generated through the interaction of these three components.

CSR Corporate Social Responsibility is the responsibility of a company to tackle environmental and social problems. It's a business model as a means to operate in positive and impactful ways toward society and the environment.

Carbon Credit Payment to a company for reducing their greenhouse gas emissions and carbon footprint. One credit allows for emitting one ton of carbon dioxide or other greenhouse gasses.

Community Benefit Society A business with the objective of improving the community through investment of profits and other practices.

Community Development Finance Institutions Businesses that provide financial services to underserved impoverished communities to promote economic development. They create opportunities for groups and individuals to acquire economic resources and secure adequate necessities.

Community Interest Company Social enterprises that use funds to promote initiatives within a community. These companies use their profits or surpluses to reinvest or support social initiatives. In other words, they aren't driven mainly by shareholder returns, like most companies today.

Crowdfunding A company's ability to raise funds for an initiative from a large number of investors through debt, equity, donations or other non-returnable contributions.

DFI Development Financial Institutions are institutions that provide capital for social finance initiatives. DFIs play a vital role financing investments and, thus, realizing goals related to ESGs and SDGs.

DIB Diversity, Inclusion, and Belonging is the value of employees from different backgrounds. Using their diverse experiences and perspectives can help a company better understand situations.

ESG   Environmental, Social, & Governance are the three areas in which a social enterprise can make an impact. Environment refers to its environmental impact through pollution, deforestation and more. Social refers to helping social issues and inequalities. Governance describes the internal diversity and makeup of the company's employees and whether or not they are driven by ethical decisions.

ESG Integration   Simply put, the integration of ESG is when a company adopts ESG ideas and practices in everyday business. The integration of ESG involves analyzing information and incorporating it into the ESG investment process.

ESG Rating   ESG ratings are given depending on how well a company promotes ESG ideas, whether positively or negatively. It's usually a measurement done on securities, funds, and companies.

ESG Reporting   Companies are required to report how much they support or hurt ESG ideas. Investors use this information to determine a company's level of sustainability and social impact considerations.

Enterprise foundation grants   Grants for nonprofit organizations or social enterprises that aim to launch their social enterprise and improve their financial stability and independence. These grants frequently serve as a conduit for social entrepreneurs to obtain revolving credit.

Environmental Factors   Issues relating to the quality and functioning of the natural environment and natural systems. These include biodiversity loss; greenhouse gas (GHG) emissions, climate change, renewable energy, energy efficiency, air, water, or resource depletion or pollution, waste management, stratospheric ozone depletion, changes in land use, ocean acidification, and changes to the nitrogen and phosphorus cycles.

Environmental Impact   A positive change in the environment through the reduction of greenhouse gasses, pollution, waste, or other means.

Environmental Management System   An Environmental Management System is a framework that helps an organization achieve its environmental goals through consistent review, evaluation, and improvement of its environmental performance.

Fiduciary duty   The obligation of trustees and other fiduciaries to maximize investment returns. More generally, holding such a duty would mean conducting oneself in an effort to provide financial benefit to others.

GHG Protocol   The Greenhouse Gas Protocol provides a global framework for measuring and managing emissions from private and public sector operations, value chains, products, cities, and policies to enable greenhouse gas reductions across the board.

Governance   Issues relating to the governance of companies and other investee entities. In the listed equity context, these include: board structure, size, diversity, skills and independence, executive pay, shareholder rights, stakeholder interaction, disclosure of information, business ethics, bribery and corruption, internal controls, and risk management.

GRI (Global Reporting Initiative)   The Global Reporting Initiative is an independent, international, and non-governmental organization that helps businesses and other organizations take responsibility for their impacts.

Greenwashing   The act of making false or misleading claims about the environmental benefits or performance of a product, service, technology, or organization.

Impact-Based Investing   Investments made or finance provided with the aim of generating a positive social or environmental impact alongside a financial return.

Impact Token   A group of digital tokens used on a blockchain with the specific goal of unlocking investments for projects with positive social and environmental impacts in support of the SDGs.

Microfinance   Financial tools and services are provided to low-income individuals or groups who are typically excluded from traditional banking. Microfinance provides easier access to loans through generous interest rates as well as forgiving payback periods.

Net Zero   Net zero refers to the goal of the amount of greenhouse gasses going into the atmosphere as a result of human activity being balanced by the removal of greenhouse gasses from the atmosphere.

Profit for Purpose   A profit for purpose business uses some or all of its profits to achieve social, environmental, or community benefit.

Quasi Equity   A form of debt that shares some traits with equity. The characteristics include flexible repayment terms or subordinated debt.

SDG   Social Development Goals are a collection of 17 interlinked objectives designed to serve as a "shared blueprint for peace and prosperity for people and the planet, now and into the future" from the United Nations.

SRI   Socially Responsible Investing is an investment strategy that seeks to consider both financial return and social/environmental good to bring about positive social change.

Social Enterprise   A social enterprise is a business that makes money by running to have a positive impact on the community. It reinvests all or a portion of its revenues to further that goal. include nonprofit organizations, for-profit enterprises, and everything in between.

Social Entrepreneur   An individual who establishes or supports a business in delivering a social, cultural, or environmental impact as well as a financial return.

Social Impact Bonds   an investor provides upfront capital for social services programs, and this investment is repaid—often with interest—based on the program's achievement of predetermined outcomes.

Social Investment Funds   A collection of securities that adhere to certain social, moral, religious, or environmental beliefs.

Social Investment Tax Relief   A tax incentive for individuals making an investment into an eligible charity or social enterprise.

Soft Loan   Unsecured financing provided on conditions that are more benevolent to the borrower than those obtainable from an institutional lender.

Transition Bond   Bonds that allow an issuance of debt that would go towards a company's green requirements. Such bonds can be issued by companies seeking to improve their green ratings by reducing greenhouse gas emissions.

Triple Bottom Line   The decisions of a company follow this order of importance: People, Planet, Profit. It's basically an accounting framework adapted to evaluate a company's performance from a broader, social standpoint.

VRF (Value Reporting Foundation)   The Value Reporting Foundation is a global nonprofit organization that offers a comprehensive suite of resources designed to help businesses and investors develop a shared understanding of enterprise value—how it is created, preserved, and eroded.

Value-Based Investing   An investment approach that looks at the environmental and social impact of a company's actions, products, and leaders.v

www.ingramcontent.com/pod-product-compliance
Lightning Source LLC
Chambersburg PA
CBHW070301220526
45465CB00004B/1690